EASY POP MELODIES

FOR TENOR SAX

ISBN 978-1-4803-8431-6

HAL•LEONARD®

Visit Hal Leonard Online at
www.halleonard.com

Contact us:
Hal Leonard
7777 West Bluemound Road
Milwaukee, WI 53213
Email: info@halleonard.com

In Europe, contact:
Hal Leonard Europe Limited
42 Wigmore Street
Marylebone, London, W1U 2RN
Email: info@halleonardeurope.com

In Australia, contact:
Hal Leonard Australia Pty. Ltd.
4 Lentara Court
Cheltenham, Victoria, 3192 Australia
Email: info@halleonard.com.au

ALL MY LOVING

TENOR SAX

Words and Music by JOHN LENNON
and PAUL McCARTNEY

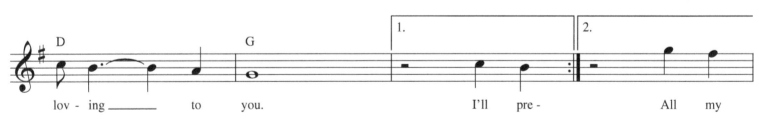

BEAUTY AND THE BEAST

from Walt Disney's BEAUTY AND THE BEAST

TENOR SAX

Lyrics by HOWARD ASHMAN
Music by ALAN MENKEN

BLOWIN' IN THE WIND

TENOR SAX

Words and Music by
BOB DYLAN

CAN YOU FEEL THE LOVE TONIGHT

from Walt Disney Pictures' THE LION KING

TENOR SAX

Music by ELTON JOHN
Lyrics by TIM RICE

There's a calm_ sur - ren - der to the rush_ of day

when the heat_ of a roll - ing wind can't be turned a - way.

An en - chant - ed mo - ment, and it sees_ me through.

It's e - nough_ for this rest - less war - ri - or just to be_ with you. And

can you feel the love ___ to - night? ___
can you feel the love ___ to - night, ___

It is where ___ we are. ___ It's e - nough
how it's laid ___ to rest? ___ It's e - nough _

___ for this wide - eyed wan - der - er that we got this far.
___ to make kings __ and vag - a - bonds be - lieve the

And ver - y best. ___

CAN'T HELP FALLING IN LOVE

TENOR SAX

Words and Music by GEORGE DAVID WEISS,
HUGO PERETTI and LUIGI CREATORE

CLOCKS

Words and Music by GUY BERRYMAN,
JON BUCKLAND, WILL CHAMPION
and CHRIS MARTIN

TENOR SAX

DAYDREAM BELIEVER

TENOR SAX

Words and Music by
JOHN STEWART

Moderately

C   Dm

Oh, I could hide 'neath the wings of the
You once thought of me as a

Em   F   C   Am

blue - bird as she sings. The six o - 'clock a - larm would nev - er
white knight on his steed. Now you know how hap - py I can

D   G   C   Dm

ring. But it rings and I rise, wipe the
be. Oh, and our good times start and end with - out

Em   F   C   Am

sleep out of my eyes. My shav - ing ra - zor's
dol - lar one to spend. But how much, ba - by,

Dm   G   C   F   G

cold ___ and it stings.)
do we real - ly need?)

Cheer up, sleep - y

Em   F   G   Am   F   C

Jean. Oh, what can it mean to a day - dream be -

F   C   Am   D   G   C

liev - er and a home - com - ing queen?

DON'T KNOW WHY

TENOR SAX

Words and Music by
JESSE HARRIS

DON'T STOP BELIEVIN'

TENOR SAX

Words and Music by STEVE PERRY,
NEAL SCHON and JONATHAN CAIN

EDELWEISS
from THE SOUND OF MUSIC

TENOR SAX

Lyrics by OSCAR HAMMERSTEIN II
Music by RICHARD RODGERS

EIGHT DAYS A WEEK

TENOR SAX

Words and Music by JOHN LENNON
and PAUL McCARTNEY

Moderately fast

1., 3. Ooh, I need your love, babe; guess you know it's true.
2. Love you ev - 'ry day, girl; al - ways on my mind.

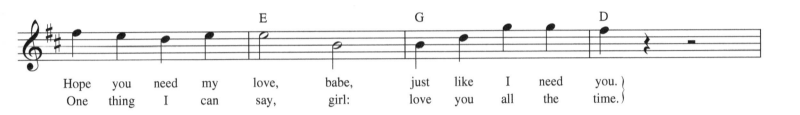

Hope you need my love, babe, just like I need you.)
One thing I can say, girl: love you all the time.)

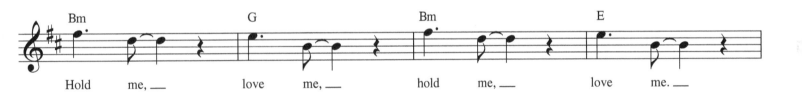

Hold me, ___ love me, ___ hold me, ___ love me. ___

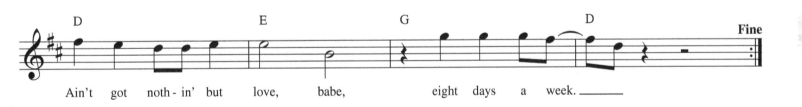

Ain't got noth - in' but love, babe, eight days a week. ___

Eight days a week I love ___ you.

Eight days a week is not e - nough to show I care. ___

EVERY BREATH YOU TAKE

TENOR SAX

Music and Lyrics by
STING

Moderately

Ev - 'ry breath you __ take,   ev - 'ry move you __ make,
Ev - 'ry move you __ make,   ev - 'ry vow you __ break,

ev - 'ry bond you break, ev - 'ry step you take, I'll be watch - ing you.
ev - 'ry smile you fake, ev - 'ry claim you stake, I'll be watch - ing you.

Ev - 'ry sin - gle __ day,   ev - 'ry word you __ say,

ev - 'ry game you play, ev - 'ry night you stay, I'll be watch ing you.

Oh, can't you __ see   you be - long to __ me?

How my poor heart _ aches _   with ev - 'ry step _ you take.

FIREFLIES

TENOR SAX

Words and Music by
ADAM YOUNG

GEORGIA ON MY MIND

TENOR SAX

Words by STUART GORRELL
Music by HOAGY CARMICHAEL

IN MY LIFE

TENOR SAX

Words and Music by JOHN LENNON
and PAUL McCARTNEY

HEY, SOUL SISTER

TENOR SAX

Words and Music by PAT MONAHAN,
ESPEN LIND and AMUND BJORKLAND

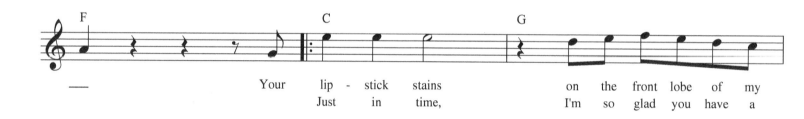

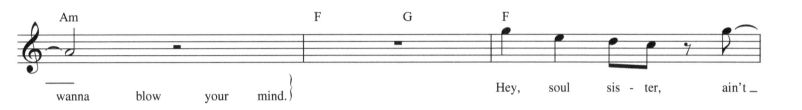

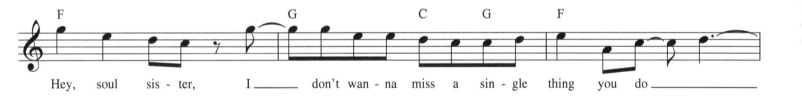

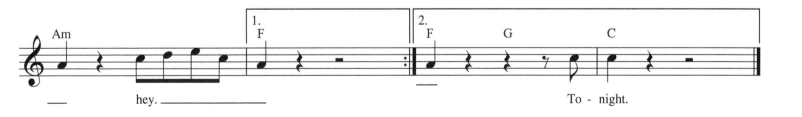

HOT N COLD

TENOR SAX

Words and Music by KATY PERRY,
MAX MARTIN and LUKASZ GOTTWALD

Moderately fast

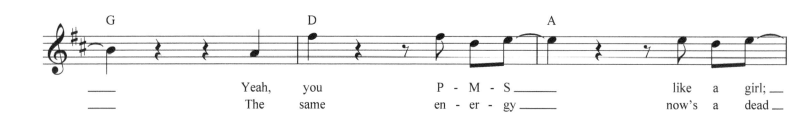

You change your mind ___ like a girl ___ chang-es clothes. ___
We used to be ___ just like twins, ___ so in sync. ___

___ Yeah, you P - M - S ___ like a girl; ___
___ The same en - er - gy ___ now's a dead ___

___ I would know. ___ And you o - ver - think, ___
___ bat - ter - y. ___ Used to laugh 'bout noth - ing; ___

al - ways speak ___ cryp - tic - 'ly. ___ I should know ___
now you're plain ___ bor - ing. ___ I should know ___

that you're ___ no good ___ for me. ___
that you're ___ not gon - na change. ___

'Cause you're hot ____ then you're cold. You're yes ____ then you're no. You're in ____

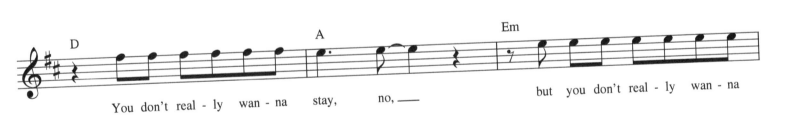

____ then you're out. You're up ____ then you're down. You're wrong ____ when it's right. It's black ____

____ and it's white. We fight, ____ we break up. We kiss, ____ we make up. ____

You don't real - ly wan - na stay, no, ____ but you don't real - ly wan - na

go. ____ You're hot ____ then you're cold. You're yes ____ then you're no. You're in ____

then you're out. You're up ____ then you're down. ____ ____ then you're down. ____

ISN'T SHE LOVELY

TENOR SAX

Words and Music by
STEVIE WONDER

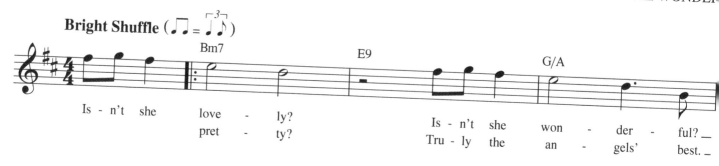

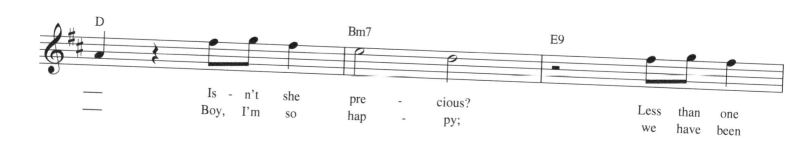

THE LETTER

TENOR SAX

Words and Music by
WAYNE CARSON THOMPSON

1., 3. Give me a tick - et for an aer - o - plane.
2. I don't care how much mon - ey I got - ta spend.

Ain't got time __ to take a
Got to get back __ to my

fast __ train.
ba - by again.

Lone - ly days are gone; __ I'm a - go - in' home. __ Oh, my

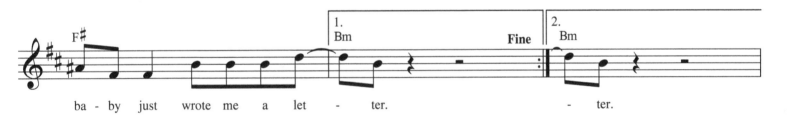

ba - by just wrote me a let - ter.

- ter.

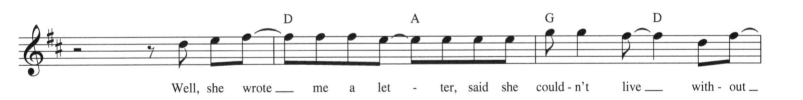

Well, she wrote __ me a let - ter, said she could - n't live __ with - out __

__ me no more.

Lis - ten, mis - ter, can't you see I

got to get back __ to my ba - by once more?

An - y - way, __ yeah.

LIKE A VIRGIN

TENOR SAX

Words and Music by BILLY STEINBERG
and TOM KELLY

THE LOOK OF LOVE

from CASINO ROYALE

TENOR SAX

Words by HAL DAVID
Music by BURT BACHARACH

LOVE ME TENDER

TENOR SAX

Words and Music by ELVIS PRESLEY
and VERA MATSON

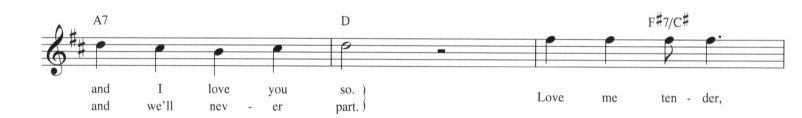

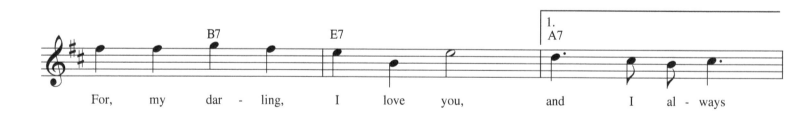

MR. TAMBOURINE MAN

TENOR SAX

Words and Music by
BOB DYLAN

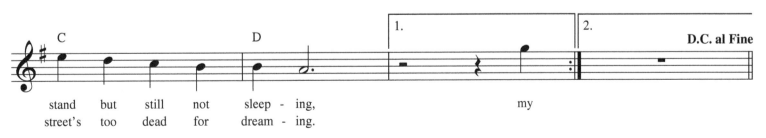

LOVE STORY

TENOR SAX

Words and Music by
TAYLOR SWIFT

Moderately

We were both young when I first saw __ you. I close my eyes __ and the

flash-back starts. __ I'm stand-ing there on a bal-co-ny in sum-mer air.

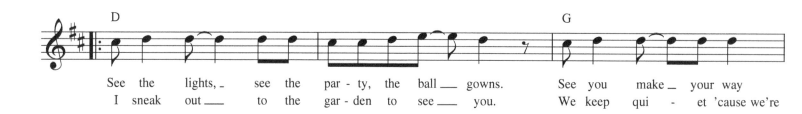

See the lights, __ see the par-ty, the ball __ gowns. See you make __ your way
I sneak out __ to the gar-den to see __ you. We keep qui - et 'cause we're

through the crowd __ and say hel - lo. Lit-tle did I _____ know
dead if they knew, __ so close your eyes, es-cape this town for a lit - tle while.

that you were Ro - me - o. You were throw-ing peb - bles, and my
'Cause you were Ro - me - o; I was the scar-let let - ter. And my

dad - dy said, "Stay a - way from Ju - li - et." __ And I was cry - ing on the stair - case,
dad - dy said, "Stay a - way from Ju - li - et." __ But you were ev - 'ry - thing to me. I was

beg - ging you, please, __ don't go. _____ And I _____ said:

Ro - me - o, take me some-where we can be a - lone. I'll be wait - ing.

All there's left to do is run. You'll be the prince and I'll be the prin - cess.

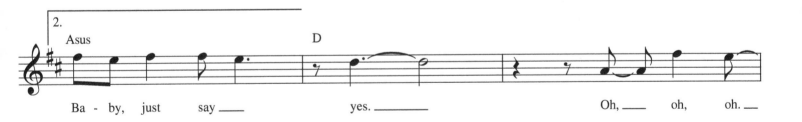

It's a love sto - ry. __ Ba - by, just say yes. So

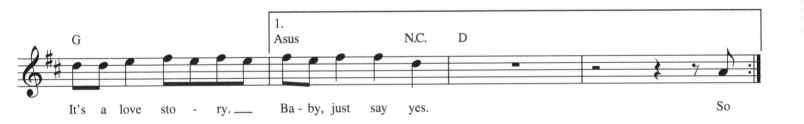

Ba - by, just say _____ yes. _____ Oh, ___ oh, oh. __

_____ Oh, ___ oh, oh, _____ oh.

'Cause we were both young when I first saw __ you. __

MOON RIVER

from the Paramount Picture BREAKFAST AT TIFFANY'S

TENOR SAX

Words by JOHNNY MERCER
Music by HENRY MANCINI

MORNING HAS BROKEN

TENOR SAX

Words by ELEANOR FARJEON
Music by CAT STEVENS

MY CHERIE AMOUR

TENOR SAX

Words and Music by STEVIE WONDER,
SYLVIA MOY and HENRY COSBY

My che - rie a - mour, ___ love - ly as a sum - mer day. ___
ca - fé, ___ or some - times on a crowd - ed street, ___

___ My che - rie a - mour, ___ dis - tant as the Milk - y Way. ___
___ I've been near ___ you, ___ but you nev - er no - ticed me. ___

___ My che - rie a - mour, ___ pret - ty lit - tle one that I ___
___ My che - rie a - mour, ___ won't you tell me, how could you ___

___ a - dore, ___ you're the on - ly girl my heart ___ beats for; ___
___ ig - nore ___ that be - hind that lit - tle smile ___ I wore, ___

how I wish that you were mine. ___ In a La la

la la ___ la la, la la la la ___ la la. La la

la la ___ la la, la la la la ___ la la.

MY GIRL

TENOR SAX

Words and Music by WILLIAM "SMOKEY" ROBINSON
and RONALD WHITE

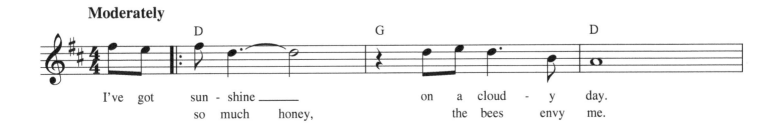

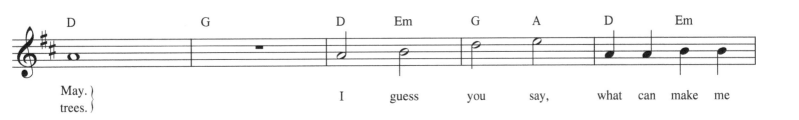

MY FAVORITE THINGS
from THE SOUND OF MUSIC

TENOR SAX

Lyrics by OSCAR HAMMERSTEIN II
Music by RICHARD RODGERS

Brightly

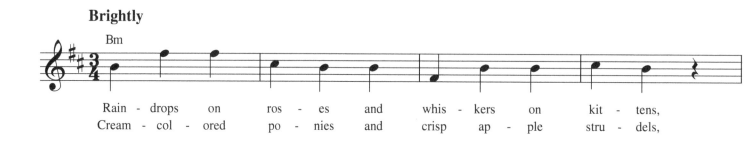

Rain - drops on ros - es and whis - kers on kit - tens,
Cream - col - ored po - nies and crisp ap - ple stru - dels,

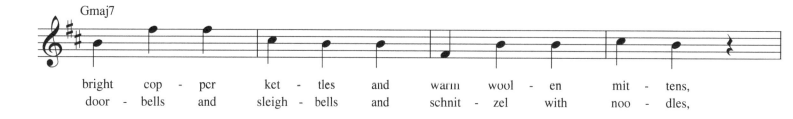

bright cop - per ket - tles and warm wool - en mit - tens,
door - bells and sleigh - bells and schnit - zel with noo - dles,

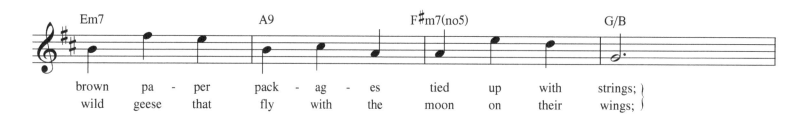

brown pa - per pack - ag - es tied up with strings;)
wild geese that fly with the moon on their wings;)

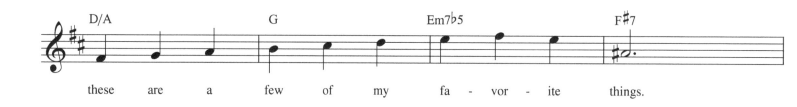

these are a few of my fa - vor - ite things.

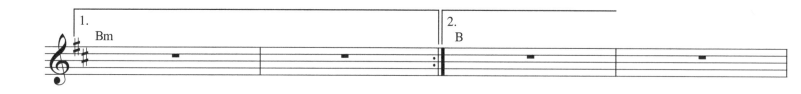

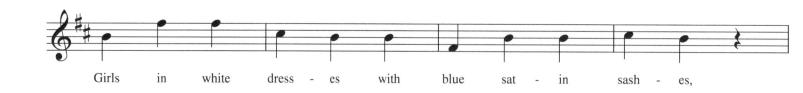

Girls in white dress - es with blue sat - in sash - es,

MY HEART WILL GO ON
(Love Theme from 'Titanic')
from the Paramount and Twentieth Century Fox Motion Picture TITANIC

TENOR SAX

Music by JAMES HORNER
Lyric by WILL JENNINGS

NIGHTS IN WHITE SATIN

TENOR SAX

Words and Music by
JUSTIN HAYWARD

NOWHERE MAN

TENOR SAX

Words and Music by JOHN LENNON
and PAUL McCARTNEY

PUFF THE MAGIC DRAGON

TENOR SAX

Words and Music by LENNY LIPTON
and PETER YARROW

RAINDROPS KEEP FALLIN' ON MY HEAD
from BUTCH CASSIDY AND THE SUNDANCE KID

TENOR SAX

Lyric by HAL DAVID
Music by BURT BACHARACH

SCARBOROUGH FAIR/CANTICLE

TENOR SAX

Arrangement and Original Counter Melody by PAUL SIMON
and ARTHUR GARFUNKEL

SOMEWHERE OUT THERE

from AN AMERICAN TAIL

TENOR SAX

Music by BARRY MANN and JAMES HORNER
Lyric by CYNTHIA WEIL

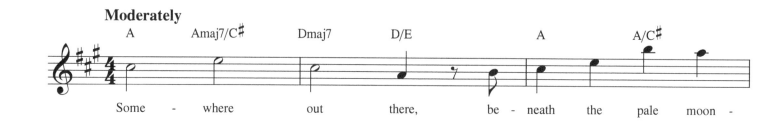

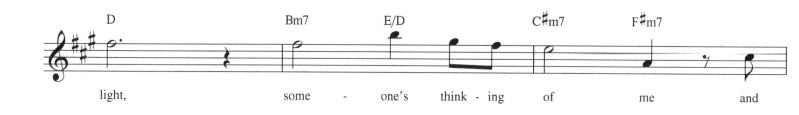

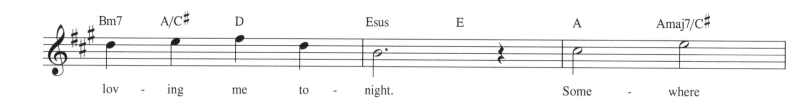

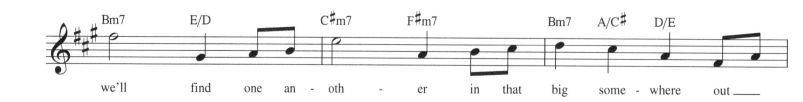

there. And e - ven though I know how ver - y far a - part we are, it

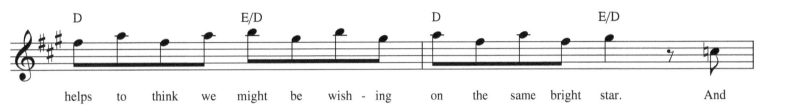

helps to think we might be wish - ing on the same bright star. And

when the night wind starts to sing that lone - some lull - a - by, it

helps to think we're sleep - ing un - der - neath the same big sky.

Some - where out there, if love can see us

through, then we'll be to - geth - er some - where

out there, out where dreams come true.

THE SOUND OF MUSIC

from THE SOUND OF MUSIC

TENOR SAX

Lyrics by OSCAR HAMMERSTEIN II
Music by RICHARD RODGERS

Moderately

The hills are a-live with the sound of mu - sic, _____ with

songs they have sung for a thou-sand years. _____ The

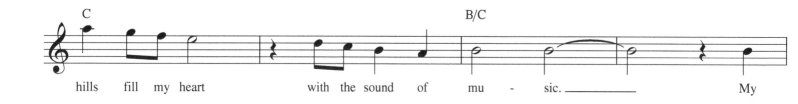

hills fill my heart with the sound of mu - sic. _____ My

heart wants to sing ev-'ry song it hears. _____ My heart wants to

beat like the wings of the birds that rise from the lake to the

trees. My heart wants to sigh like a chime that flies from a

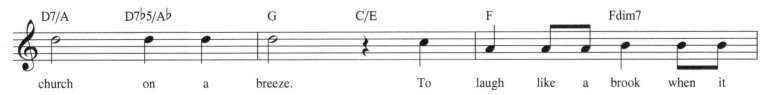

church on a breeze. To laugh like a brook when it

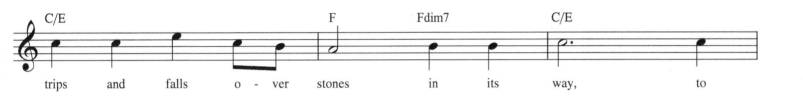

trips and falls o - ver stones in its way, to

sing through the night like a lark who is learn - ing to pray. I

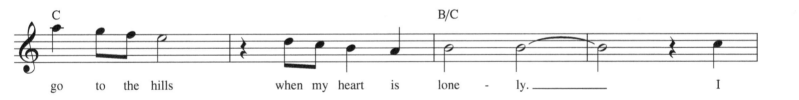

go to the hills when my heart is lone - ly. _____ I

know I will hear what I've heard be - fore. _____ My

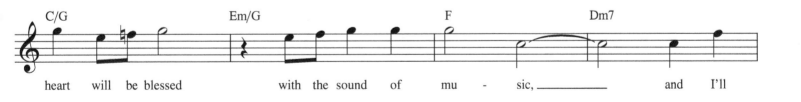

heart will be blessed with the sound of mu - sic, _____ and I'll

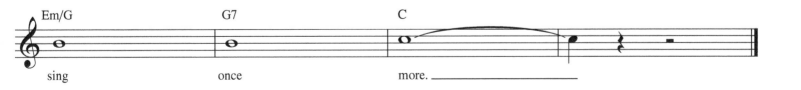

sing once more. _____

STRANGERS IN THE NIGHT

adapted from A MAN COULD GET KILLED

TENOR SAX

Words by CHARLES SINGLETON and EDDIE SNYDER
Music by BERT KAEMPFERT

SUNSHINE ON MY SHOULDERS

TENOR SAX

Words by JOHN DENVER
Music by JOHN DENVER, MIKE TAYLOR
and DICK KNISS

SWEET CAROLINE

TENOR SAX

Words and Music by
NEIL DIAMOND

Moderately

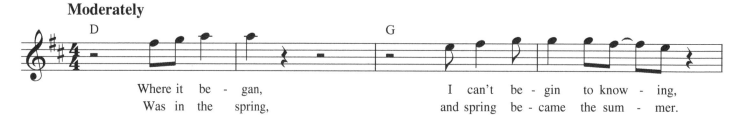

Where it be - gan, I can't be - gin to know - ing,
Was in the spring, and spring be - came the sum - mer.

but then, I know it's grow - ing strong.
Who'd have be - lieved you'd come _ a -

long. Hands, _____ touch-ing hands, _____

reach-ing out, touch-ing me, touch-ing you. _____

Sweet Car - o - line, ___ good times nev - er seemed so
I've been in - clined ___ to be - lieve they nev - er

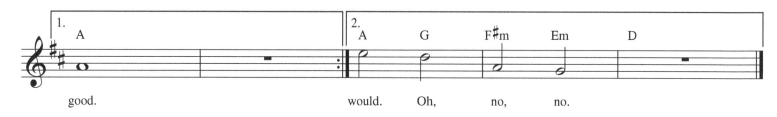

good. would. Oh, no, no.

TILL THERE WAS YOU
from Meredith Willson's THE MUSIC MAN

TENOR SAX

By MEREDITH WILLSON

THE TIMES THEY ARE A-CHANGIN'

TENOR SAX

Words and Music by
BOB DYLAN

UNCHAINED MELODY

TENOR SAX

Lyric by HY ZARET
Music by ALEX NORTH

TOMORROW
from The Musical Production ANNIE

TENOR SAX

Lyric by MARTIN CHARNIN
Music by CHARLES STROUSE

Moderately fast

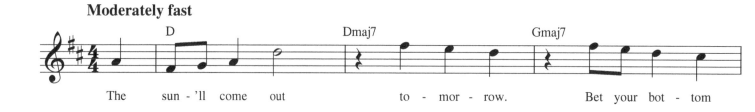

The sun - 'll come out to - mor - row. Bet your bot - tom

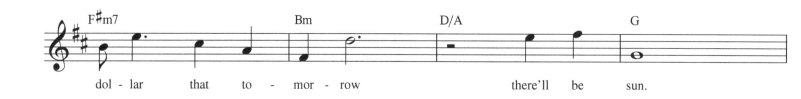

dol - lar that to - mor - row there'll be sun.

Just think - ing a - bout to - mor - row clears a - way the

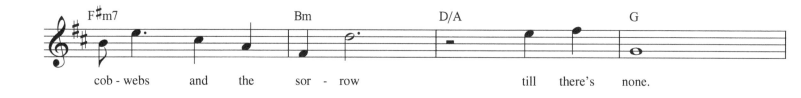

cob - webs and the sor - row till there's none.

When I'm stuck with a day that's gray and lone - ly,

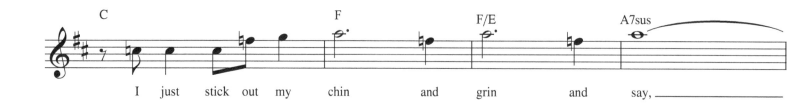

I just stick out my chin and grin and say, ___

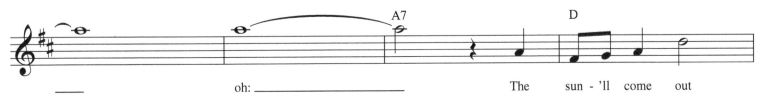

_____ oh: _____ The sun - 'll come out

to - mor - row, so you got - ta hang on till to - mor - row,

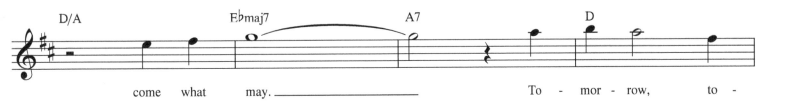

come what may. _____ To - mor - row, to -

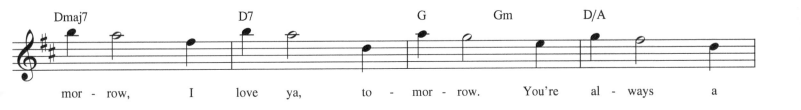

mor - row, I love ya, to - mor - row. You're al - ways a

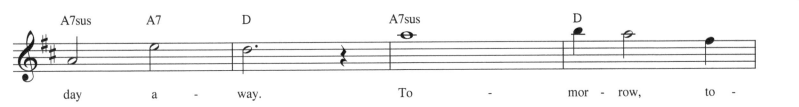

day a - way. To - mor - row, to -

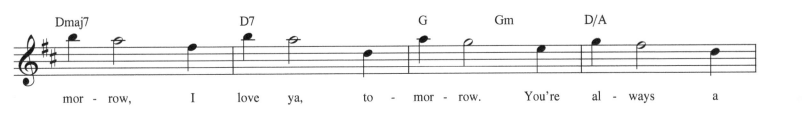

mor - row, I love ya, to - mor - row. You're al - ways a

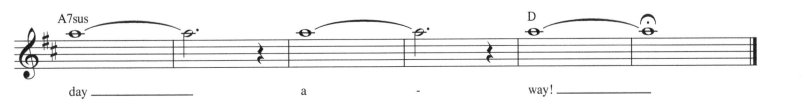

day _____ a - way! _____

VIVA LA VIDA

TENOR SAX

Words and Music by GUY BERRYMAN,
JON BUCKLAND, WILL CHAMPION
and CHRIS MARTIN

Moderately

I used to rule the world. ___ Seas would rise when I gave the word. ___

___ Now in the morn-ing I sleep a - lone, ___ sweep the

streets I used to own. ___

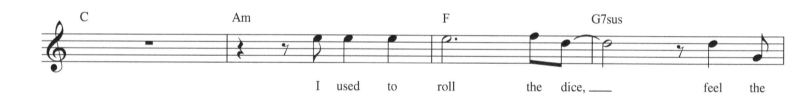

I used to roll the dice, ___ feel the

fear in my en - e - my's eyes, ___ lis - ten as the crowd ___ would sing, ___

___ "Now the old king is dead; ___ long live the king." One min - ute I

held the key, ___ next the walls were closed on

me. And I dis - cov - ered that my cas - tles stand ___ up - on

pil - lars of salt ___ and pil - lars of sand. ___ I hear Je - ru - sa - lem bells ___

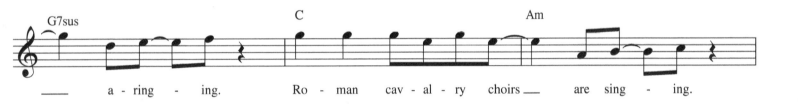

___ a - ring - ing. Ro - man cav - al - ry choirs ___ are sing - ing.

Be my mir - ror, my sword ___ and shield, ___ my mis - sion - ar - ies in a for -

- eign field. ___ For some rea - son I can't ___ ex - plain, ___

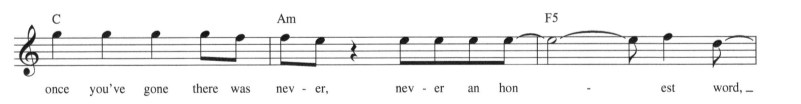

once you've gone there was nev - er, nev - er an hon - est word, ___

___ and that was when I ruled the world. ___

WE ARE THE WORLD

TENOR SAX

Words and Music by LIONEL RICHIE
and MICHAEL JACKSON

Moderately

There comes a time ___ when we heed a cer - tain call, ___ when the
We can't go on ___ pre - tend - ing day ___ by day ___ that some -

world must come to - geth - er as one. There are peo -
one some - where will soon make a change. We are all ___

- ple dy - ing, oh, and it's time ___ to lend a hand to life,
___ a part ___ of God's ___ great ___ big fam - i - ly, and the

1.
the great - est gift ___ of all. ___
truth, you know love is all ___ we

2.
need. ___

___ We are the world, ___ we are the chil - dren.

We are the ones ___ who make a bright-er day, ___ so let's ___ start giv - ing.

There's a choice we're mak - ing; ___ we're sav - ing our ___ own lives. ___

___ It's true: ___ we make a bet - ter day, ___ just you ___ and me.

WHAT A WONDERFUL WORLD

Tenor Sax

Words and Music by GEORGE DAVID WEISS
and BOB THIELE

WONDERWALL

TENOR SAX

Words and Music by
NOEL GALLAGHER

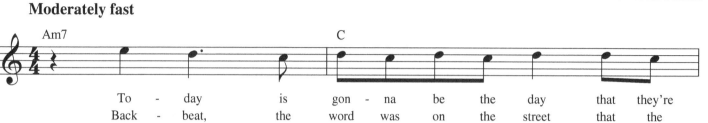

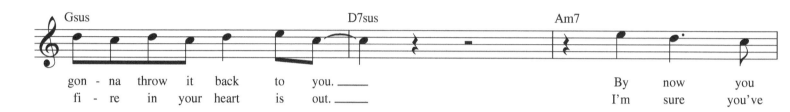

To - day is gon - na be the day that they're
Back - beat, is the word was on the street that the

gon - na throw it back to you. ___ By now you
fi - re in your heart is out. ___ I'm sure you've

should - 've some - how re - al - ized what you got - ta do. ___
heard it all be - fore, but you never real - ly had a doubt. ___

I don't be - lieve ___ that an - y - bod - y feels the way I do ___

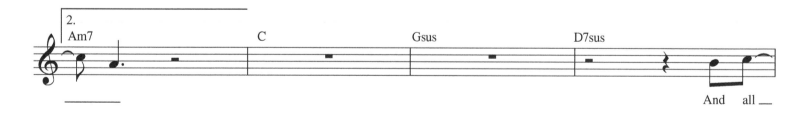

__ a - bout you now. ___

2.
___ And all ___

___ the roads ___ we have ___ to walk ___ are wind - ing, and all ___

the lights _ that lead ___ us there _ are blind - ing.

There are man - y things ___ that I ____ would like to say to you, _

___ but I don't know how. _____

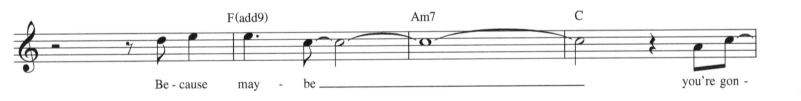

Be - cause may - be _____ you're gon -

- na be the one that saves me, _____ and

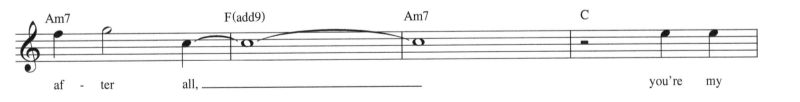

af - ter all, _____ you're my

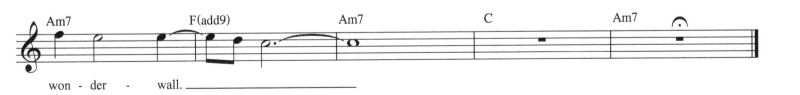

won - der - wall. _____

YOU ARE THE SUNSHINE OF MY LIFE

TENOR SAX

Words and Music by
STEVIE WONDER

Brightly

You are the sun - shine of __ my life. __
You are the ap - ple of __ my eye. __

That's why I'll al - ways be __ a - round. __
For - ev - er you'll __ stay in __ my heart. __

I feel like this __ is the __ be - gin - ning, __

though I've loved you __ for a thou - sand years. __

And if I thought __ our love __ was end - ing, __ I'd find __

D.C. al Fine
(take repeat)

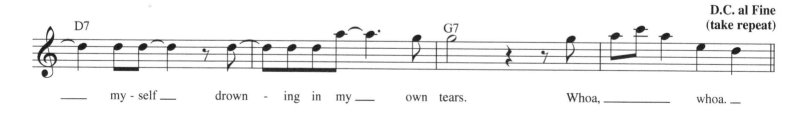

__ my - self __ drown - ing in my __ own tears. Whoa, __ whoa. __

YOU'VE GOT A FRIEND

TENOR SAX

Words and Music by
CAROLE KING

Audio Access Included HAL•LEONARD

EASY INSTRUMENTAL PLAY-ALONG

- Perfect for beginning players
- Carefully edited to include only the notes and rhythms that students learn in the first months playing their instrument

- Great-sounding demonstration and play-along tracks
- Audio tracks can be accessed online for download or streaming, using the unique code inside the book

DISNEY
Book with Online Audio Tracks

The Ballad of Davy Crockett • Can You Feel the Love Tonight • Candle on the Water • I Just Can't Wait to Be King • The Medallion Calls • Mickey Mouse March • Part of Your World • Whistle While You Work • You Can Fly! You Can Fly! You Can Fly! • You'll Be in My Heart (Pop Version).

00122184	Flute	$9.99
00122185	Clarinet	$9.99
00122186	Alto Sax	$9.99
00122187	Tenor Sax	$9.99
00122188	Trumpet	$9.99
00122189	Horn	$9.99
00122190	Trombone	$9.99
00122191	Violin	$9.99
00122192	Viola	$9.99
00122193	Cello	$9.99
00122194	Keyboard Percussion	$9.99

CLASSIC ROCK
Book with Online Audio Tracks

Another One Bites the Dust • Born to Be Wild • Brown Eyed Girl • Dust in the Wind • Every Breath You Take • Fly like an Eagle • I Heard It Through the Grapevine • I Shot the Sheriff • Oye Como Va • Up Around the Bend.

00122195	Flute	$9.99
00122196	Clarinet	$9.99
00122197	Alto Sax	$9.99
00122198	Tenor Sax	$9.99
00122201	Trumpet	$9.99
00122202	Horn	$9.99
00122203	Trombone	$9.99
00122205	Violin	$9.99
00122206	Viola	$9.99
00122207	Cello	$9.99
00122208	Keyboard Percussion	$9.99

CLASSICAL THEMES
Book with Online Audio Tracks

Can Can • Carnival of Venice • Finlandia • Largo from Symphony No. 9 ("New World") • Morning • Musette in D Major • Ode to Joy • Spring • Symphony No. 1 in C Minor, Fourth Movement Excerpt • Trumpet Voluntary.

00123108	Flute	$9.99
00123109	Clarinet	$9.99
00123110	Alto Sax	$9.99
00123111	Tenor Sax	$9.99
00123112	Trumpet	$9.99
00123113	Horn	$9.99
00123114	Trombone	$9.99
00123115	Violin	$9.99
00123116	Viola	$9.99
00123117	Cello	$9.99
00123118	Keyboard Percussion	$9.99

CHRISTMAS CAROLS
Book with Online Audio Tracks

Angels We Have Heard on High • Christ Was Born on Christmas Day • Come, All Ye Shepherds • Come, Thou Long-Expected Jesus • Good Christian Men, Rejoice • Jingle Bells • Jolly Old St. Nicholas • Lo, How a Rose E'er Blooming • On Christmas Night • Up on the Housetop.

00130363	Flute	$9.99
00130364	Clarinet	$9.99
00130365	Alto Sax	$9.99
00130366	Tenor Sax	$9.99
00130367	Trumpet	$9.99
00130368	Horn	$9.99
00130369	Trombone	$9.99
00130370	Violin	$9.99
00130371	Viola	$9.99
00130372	Cello	$9.99
00130373	Keyboard Percussion	$9.99

POP FAVORITES
Book with Online Audio Tracks

Achy Breaky Heart (Don't Tell My Heart) • I'm a Believer • Imagine • Jailhouse Rock • La Bamba • Louie, Louie • Ob-La-Di, Ob-La-Da • Splish Splash • Stand by Me • Yellow Submarine.

00232231	Flute	$9.99
00232232	Clarinet	$9.99
00232233	Alto Sax	$9.99
00232234	Tenor Sax	$9.99
00232235	Trumpet	$9.99
00232236	Horn	$9.99
00232237	Trombone	$9.99
00232238	Violin	$9.99
00232239	Viola	$9.99
00232240	Cello	$9.99
00233296	Keyboard Percussion	$9.99

HAL•LEONARD®
www.halleonard.com